Original title:
Happiness Quest

Copyright © 2024 Creative Arts Management OÜ
All rights reserved.

Author: Clement Portlander
ISBN HARDBACK: 978-9916-88-188-0
ISBN PAPERBACK: 978-9916-88-189-7

A Quest for Inner Sunshine

In shadows deep, where doubts may linger,
I seek a light that warms the soul.
Through winding paths, I clutch my finger,
On dreams that whisper, make me whole.

With every step, a breath of hope,
I chase the rays that break the gloom.
In every heart, a way to cope,
I'll find the spark that starts to bloom.

The clouds may gather, fierce and gray,
Yet in my chest, a fire burns bright.
I'll turn the night to dawning day,
Embracing all, the dark and light.

So here I stand, I will not wane,
For inside me lies endless skies.
With courage bold, I'll face the rain,
In search of self, my spirit flies.

The Language of Laughter

Laughter dances in the air,
A melody that's light and free.
It bridges hearts beyond compare,
In joy, we find our unity.

Giggles, chuckles, echo bright,
Each sound a spark, a fleeting grace.
With every grin, the world feels right,
In laughter's warm and sweet embrace.

Moments that Sparkle

Twilight whispers secrets rare,
Stars appear like dreams set free.
In fleeting glances, magic's there,
A tapestry of memory.

The sun dips low, a vibrant hue,
While shadows dance and spirits soar.
These moments shared, forever true,
Glisten with love, forevermore.

The Alchemy of Bliss

In stillness, joy begins to rise,
A touch of peace within the soul.
Transmuting moments into sighs,
Where laughter plays a vital role.

Golden rays on morning dew,
Each heartbeat sings a sweet refrain.
In quiet joy, we find what's true,
A treasure born from love and pain.

Flowers in Full Bloom

Petals open, colors bright,
Nature's brushstrokes spread delight.
In gardens where the sunlight streams,
Beauty flourishes, like our dreams.

Fragrance dances on the breeze,
Whispers soft of love and grace.
A symphony among the trees,
Life's palette paints a sacred space.

The Charm of Ordinary Days

In the quiet of dawn, light peeks through,
Coffee brews gently, a warm morning cue.
Whispers of nature call out in the breeze,
Moments of stillness, heart finds its ease.

Children play games, laughter fills the air,
Simple joys linger, beyond compare.
A book in my hands, a soft, cozy chair,
Ordinary wonders, love everywhere.

Glimmers of Gratitude

Each breath a blessing, a gift to behold,
Sunset on horizons, painted in gold.
Grateful heartbeats dance with the stars,
Finding joy in memories, near and far.

The warmth of a smile, the touch of a hand,
Tiny moments build the life that we planned.
Nature's soft whispers, stories unfold,
Glimmers of gratitude, priceless as gold.

The Echo of Laughter

In a room filled with cheer, echoes ring clear,
Laughter like music, a symphony dear.
Eyes sparkling bright, hearts open wide,
In these shared moments, we love and abide.

Stories of old bring smiles and delight,
Memories woven in the soft evening light.
Laughter dances freely, lifting the soul,
In the warmth of each chuckle, we find ourselves whole.

Luminous Days Ahead

Hope glimmers softly, a beacon so bright,
Carrying dreams into the heart of the night.
With each rising sun, new paths to explore,
Luminous days wait, with wonders in store.

Tender moments promise joy in their grace,
Every step forward, a new, warm embrace.
With courage as our guide, we'll journey and play,
Luminous futures await, lighting the way.

Reverberations of Joy

In the laughter, melodies play,
Colors dance in bright array.
Hearts united, spirits soar,
Echoing love forevermore.

Through the chaos, we find peace,
Moments cherished, never cease.
With each heartbeat, joy ignites,
Lighting up the darkest nights.

The Wind Beneath My Wings

You lift me high, like a dream,
Gentle whispers in the beam.
Through the storms, your strength I feel,
A silent vow, our fate is sealed.

Every challenge, by your side,
In your warmth, I brave the tide.
With your love, I find my way,
Together, brighter every day.

Sunlit Pathways

Golden rays on endless trails,
Nature's beauty never pales.
Each step forward, hope unfolds,
Stories waiting to be told.

With your hand, I walk with grace,
Heartfelt joy in every space.
Life's an adventure we embrace,
Sunlit moments, a warm embrace.

Dreams in Technicolor

Vibrant hues in every thought,
A canvas draped with what is sought.
In our minds, we paint the skies,
Where the whispered longing lies.

Every vision bold and bright,
Guides us through the still of night.
In the tapestry we weave,
Dreams in color, we believe.

Unveiling the Spark

In shadows deep, a glimmer shines,
A flicker born, in heart it twines.
With every breath, the light expands,
Awakening dreams, through gentle hands.

A quiet whisper, the soul's embrace,
In moments still, we find our place.
Life's tender notes, a symphony,
Unveils the spark, we long to see.

Enchanted by Bliss

In fields of gold, where daisies dance,
The breeze, a song, in sweet romance.
With laughter's grace, the heart takes flight,
In every color, the world ignites.

Beneath the stars, we share a dream,
Where moonlit paths and wishes gleam.
Each whispered hope, a gentle kiss,
In this embrace, we find our bliss.

Steps on the Bright Side

With every step, the dawn unfolds,
A journey bright, where hope beholds.
Through trials faced, our spirits soar,
Together we walk, forever more.

The sun arises, casting light,
In shadows past, we find our might.
Embracing joy, we choose to glide,
In every heartbeat, on the bright side.

A Tapestry of Merriment

In laughter's thread, the stories weave,
A tapestry, in hearts we believe.
With colors bold, and patterns bright,
We dance through life, in pure delight.

Each stitch a joy, in moments shared,
Through every challenge, love declared.
A woven bond, forever strong,
In merriment, we all belong.

Chasing Chasing Rainbows

In the sky, colors intertwine,
Dreams unfurl like ribbons fine.
Footsteps follow where light bends,
Hope and joy, the heart transcends.

Across the fields of golden hue,
We chase the light, our spirits true.
With every turn, new sights we find,
A treasure trove, the heart aligned.

The Mirror of Kindness

A gentle smile can change a day,
Reflections of love in every way.
In the eyes, a story glows,
Kindness blooms where compassion flows.

Let the heart guide every deed,
In the silence, let kindness lead.
For every echo of a kind word,
Can lift the soul, like wings of a bird.

The Skyline of Serenity

Above the world, the skyline gleams,
A haven found in soft daydreams.
Clouds drift lazily, peace in tow,
In every breath, a gentle flow.

Mountains stand tall, guardians proud,
Whispers of nature, soft and loud.
Beneath the sky, we find our place,
In the embrace of calm and grace.

A Voyage of Glee

Set sail with joy, the winds embrace,
Adventure calls, our hearts will race.
Across the waves, we journey far,
Guided by dreams, beneath the stars.

With every laugh, we chart our course,
Together we grow, an endless force.
The horizon beckons, bright and free,
In this voyage, love's decree.

The Path of Playfulness

In fields where laughter roams so free,
Joyful spirits find their glee.
Chasing dreams like butterflies,
The world is bright under sunny skies.

With every leap and bound so spry,
Children's giggles lift us high.
Embracing life in vibrant hue,
The path of play is tried and true.

The Essence of Light-heartedness

A dance of joy beneath the sun,
Where worries fade, and hearts are won.
In every smile, a story gleams,
Life unfolds like tender dreams.

With laughter's echo in the air,
We breeze through moments without care.
Each simple joy, a treasure vast,
In light-heartedness, our shadows past.

Glimpses of the Good Life

In morning light, the world awakes,
With gentle warmth, the heart it takes.
Simple pleasures, a cup of tea,
Glimpses of life so beautifully free.

With friends who share our laughter's tune,
Beneath the glow of a silver moon.
Moments cherished, like colors bright,
In the canvas of life, pure delight.

The Tides of Tranquility

On shores where whispers kiss the sand,
Gentle waves caress the land.
In silence deep, our spirits roam,
Finding peace, we feel at home.

The ebb and flow, a soothing sigh,
Beneath the vast and open sky.
In tranquility, we find our way,
A perfect end to every day.

Blossoms of Bliss

In gardens where the sunlit glows,
Petals dance in fragrant rows.
Whispers soft beneath the trees,
Nature sings with gentle breeze.

Colors bright, a vivid dream,
Joy reflected in the stream.
Every bloom, a tale to weave,
In their beauty, we believe.

Morning dew like diamonds shine,
Hearts entwined in love's design.
In this place where laughter lives,
Blossoms of joy, the soul it gives.

Footsteps light on paths of green,
Life is rich and evergreen.
In the tender touch of spring,
Blissful songs of hope we sing.

A Journey Beyond the Clouds

Upon the wings of silver skies,
We find the dreams where freedom lies.
Floating high, beyond the trees,
Whispers carried on the breeze.

Mountains rise, and rivers flow,
In this realm where wonders grow.
Every star, a guiding light,
Leading us through endless night.

Adventure calls with gentle sound,
In the sky, our hearts are bound.
Through the realms of sheer delight,
We journey on, embracing flight.

Together we will brave the height,
Chasing shadows, seeking light.
Beyond the clouds, we'll find our way,
In the dawn of a brand new day.

Echoes of Enchantment

In the forest where shadows play,
Mystic echoes call and sway.
Soft as whispers from the past,
Moments linger, spells are cast.

Moonlight drapes the ancient trees,
Carrying secrets in the breeze.
With every step, a story told,
Of magic woven, dreams unfold.

Hearts awaken to the night,
Guided softly by the light.
In this space of pure romance,
Life takes on a joyful dance.

With each note, the air enchants,
In the rhythm, nature chants.
Harmony in every sound,
Echoes of life's beauty found.

Trails of Tranquility

Along the path where silence dwells,
Nature's peace, a soothing spell.
Gentle streams and rustling leaves,
In this stillness, the heart believes.

Mountains whisper ancient tales,
Carrying dreams on tranquil sails.
With every step, the spirit soars,
Finding solace in nature's shores.

Sunsets paint the skies in hues,
Moments captured, calmness ensues.
Every breath a gift so sweet,
In this haven, our souls meet.

With twilight's grace upon our face,
We embrace the tranquil space.
On these trails of pure delight,
We walk together into the night.

The Art of Grinning

A smile is worth a thousand words,
It dances bright as morning birds.
In every glance, a spark may gleam,
Grinning is the heart's pure theme.

Through trials faced, through shadows passed,
In laughter's light, our fears are cast.
With each small joy that we reveal,
The art of grinning helps us heal.

Painted Skies of Elation

In twilight hues, the heavens sigh,
With strokes of gold, the day bids bye.
Each cloud a canvas, dreams take flight,
The painted skies bring pure delight.

Within the colors, stories weave,
A tapestry that bids us believe.
In every shade, a secret glows,
In painted skies, our spirit flows.

The Melody of Being

In quiet moments, life unfolds,
A gentle rhythm, truth beholds.
Each heartbeat sings a timeless tune,
The melody of life, a boon.

In joy and sorrow, notes entwine,
Together weaving fate divine.
With every breath, a song we share,
The melody of being, rare.

Sails of Serenity

Upon the sea of calm we glide,
With sails of peace, we drift and bide.
The winds of hope, they gently steer,
In sails of serenity, no fear.

Through swells of change, we find our way,
In stillness lies a brighter day.
With every wave, let worries cease,
On sails of serenity, we find peace.

The Dance of Contentment

In the quiet of a gentle breeze,
Joy twirls softly with ease.
Moments linger, hearts align,
Peaceful whispers, love's design.

Laughter echoes through the trees,
Worries fade, melting like breeze.
Each step taken, light and free,
Grateful souls, a harmony.

Together we sway under the stars,
Boundless dreams, no distant bars.
In this dance, our spirits soar,
In contentment's arms, we explore.

So let us twirl, embrace the night,
In the dance of life, pure delight.
With every beat, we find our way,
In laughter's glow, forever stay.

Canvas of Cheer

A splash of color, bold and bright,
Paints the world in pure delight.
Joyful strokes across the ground,
A vibrant melody, all around.

Sunshine smiles through the clouds,
Cheerful whispers in lively crowds.
Brushes dance with a joyous flair,
Creating dreams in the open air.

Every hue tells a story grand,
Of love and laughter, hand in hand.
In this canvas, hearts converge,
Painting happiness, we emerge.

Let's celebrate each color's song,
In a world where we all belong.
With every shade, our spirits soar,
On this canvas, forever more.

The Lightness of Living

In morning's glow, the world awakes,
A gentle breeze, the heart it takes.
Feet dancing on the dewy grass,
Moments fleeting, but none shall pass.

Clouds drift softly, a sailing dream,
Life flows by like a flowing stream.
With laughter ringing through the air,
Every heartbeat, free of care.

Simplicity shines in every glance,
Inviting joy in life's sweet dance.
Like butterflies, we float and sway,
In the lightness of living, we play.

So let us cherish, breathe it in,
The beauty found in all that's been.
With open hearts and spirits bright,
We live with love, we live in light.

A Symphony of Smiles

In the morning's soft embrace,
A symphony begins to trace.
Notes of laughter fill the air,
Smiles exchanged with love and care.

Each grin a melody, sweet and clear,
Resonating for all to hear.
Together we weave a joyful song,
In this harmony, we all belong.

Through the highs and the gentle lows,
The symphony of life brightly glows.
With every laugh, the heart expands,
Creating joy that understands.

So lift your voice, let spirits rise,
In this concert of hopeful skies.
In unity, we find our style,
Embracing life with every smile.

Portraits of Positivity

In hues of joy, we find our spark,
Each moment shines, erasing dark.
Laughter dances on the breeze,
A canvas bright, our hearts at ease.

With every smile, a story glows,
In kindness shared, our spirit grows.
We paint our lives with care and grace,
In this warm light, we find our place.

Embrace the dawn with open hands,
Together, strong, as love expands.
In little things, the beauty swells,
In positive thoughts, our hope compels.

So let us cherish every hue,
In portraits true, in all we do.
A tapestry of hearts combined,
In unity, our peace we find.

A Leaf in the Wind

A single leaf, it twirls and spins,
Carried forth by gentle winds.
In flight, it dances, free and bold,
A fleeting tale of nature told.

Through shadows cast, it finds its way,
Each twist and turn, a bright display.
It whispers secrets to the skies,
And marvels at the world's replies.

With every gust, new paths unfold,
Embracing change, a sight to behold.
In every drift, there's peace we gain,
As life's own rhythm we sustain.

So let us learn from winds that bring,
The wisdom found in shifting things.
Like leaves that float on currents wide,
In trust, we soar, our hearts our guide.

The Smile of Tomorrow

A tender smile breaks through the gray,
It lights the path, it guides the way.
With hope ignited in every beam,
Tomorrow whispers, chase your dream.

Through trials faced and lessons learned,
In every heart, a fire burned.
The promise blooms like flowers bright,
In every dawn, a chance for flight.

With open arms, the future calls,
In laughter shared, our spirit sprawls.
Each moment crafted, pure and true,
In smiles exchanged, we start anew.

So lift your gaze to skies above,
In every heartbeat, feel the love.
For in each smile that we bestow,
Lies the radiant light of tomorrow.

Secrets Beneath the Surface

In quiet depths where shadows blend,
A world awaits, around the bend.
The whispers soft of stories spun,
In silence held, but not undone.

Beneath the waves, the currents hide,
The echoes of the heart's deep tide.
In hidden realms, the truth resides,
In layers thick, where mystery guides.

As secrets flow with ebb and flow,
A dance of thoughts, a silent show.
We delve beneath, unearth the gold,
In every secret, wisdom told.

So let us venture, brave and bold,
To what the surface can't unfold.
In depths of what we cannot see,
Lie threads of life, our destiny.

Lanterns of Laughter

In the night sky, lanterns glow,
Whispers of joy, soft and low.
Children's giggles float on air,
Crafted with love, moments rare.

Balloons dance high, colors bright,
Filling our hearts with pure delight.
Under the stars, we share our dreams,
Everything's better, or so it seems.

Stories unfold, beneath the moon,
Echoing laughter, a sweet tune.
Together we hold, memories sweet,
Time stands still, our hearts skip a beat.

As the lanterns drift away,
We cherish this magical day.
In the night's embrace, we stand tall,
For in laughter's light, we have it all.

The Cartographer of Contentment

With ink and quill, a map is drawn,
In the quiet dawn, a new day born.
Each line a path to joy and peace,
A journey where worries cease.

Lakes of laughter, hills of cheer,
Crossing valleys, holding dear.
In every corner, a treasure hides,
In the heart, true joy abides.

Mountains rise, touching the sky,
Landing where peaceful moments lie.
A compass guides, the heart's delight,
Through the day, into the night.

The world unfolds, a precious scroll,
Charting the way to the soul's true goal.
In this map, let us reside,
Together, in joy, side by side.

A Voyage through Radiant Waters

Set sail on waves that glitter bright,
Beneath the sun's warm, golden light.
With every splash, a story to tell,
In radiant waters, we dance and swell.

Seagulls cry, the breeze takes flight,
Guiding our boat into the night.
Stars above begin to gleam,
A voyage here feels like a dream.

As the tide bids us to explore,
We find treasures on every shore.
With open hearts and spirits free,
Together we weave our destiny.

In the gentle waves, we find our song,
In each moment, we truly belong.
The journey flows, our spirits rise,
In radiant waters, love never dies.

The Garden of Golden Moments

In the garden where memories bloom,
Sunlight dances, dispelling gloom.
Petals whisper of days gone by,
With every breeze, a gentle sigh.

Golden moments weave the thread,
Stories of laughter, softly spread.
Each flower holds a tale so sweet,
Every heartbeat, a cherished beat.

Under the shade of an ancient tree,
We carve our dreams, wild and free.
In this haven, love takes flight,
Filling our souls with pure delight.

As seasons change and time flows on,
In this garden, we grow strong.
Among the blooms, forever we stay,
In golden moments, come what may.

Meadows of Delight

In the meadows, flowers bloom,
Colors dance, dispelling gloom.
A gentle breeze whispers low,
Nature's joy begins to show.

Butterflies flit, wings so bright,
Chasing shadows, taking flight.
Sunlight filters through the trees,
Bringing warmth with every breeze.

Children laugh, they run and play,
In this wonder, hearts will stay.
With each step, the world feels right,
In these meadows, pure delight.

Evening falls, the day will end,
Softly now the stars descend.
Dreams arise in peaceful night,
In the meadows, love takes flight.

A Symphony of Laughter

In the park, the children play,
Joyful shouts fill up the day.
Giggles echo through the air,
Laughter's song is everywhere.

Parrots squawk and raindrops cheer,
Every moment brings us near.
With a hop and skip so free,
Life's a dance, a sweet melody.

Sunshine beams on faces bright,
Each gaze sparkling, pure delight.
Harmony in every sound,
Laughter's rhythm all around.

As the twilight starts to glow,
Hearts together, spirits flow.
In this symphony we share,
Love and laughter fill the air.

Where Dreams Take Flight

Above the clouds, dreams begin,
With open hearts, let's dive in.
Wings of hope, they soar so high,
Touching stars in the night sky.

In the stillness, visions gleam,
Whispers echo, chase your dream.
Every wish a guiding light,
Leading souls through stars so bright.

Through the valleys and the peaks,
Every heart's a song that speaks.
With each heartbeat, feel the thrill,
Where ambition dances still.

When dawn arrives, take to flight,
With the sun, let dreams ignite.
For in your heart, hope takes its place,
In the skies, find your grace.

Glimmers of Glee

Twinkling lights like stars above,
Each a little spark of love.
Shimmers dance against the night,
In the dark, they shine so bright.

Stories shared around the fire,
Glimmers warm, ignite desire.
With each laugh, we weave a thread,
Of cherished moments, softly spread.

Through the night, the music plays,
Every note a sweet embrace.
In this magic, hearts align,
Glimmers of glee, forever shine.

As dawn breaks, we won't forget,
All the joys, no need for regret.
In our souls, the warmth will stay,
Glimmers of glee, light our way.

Radiant Reflections

In the mirror of the lake,
Sun-kissed dreams awake.
Whispers of the breeze,
Dance among the trees.

Shimmering like gold,
Mysteries unfold.
Each ripple tells a tale,
As stars begin to pale.

Morning light does gleam,
Painting visions, dream.
With every gentle sway,
Reflections drift away.

Catch the fleeting grace,
In this sacred space.
Hearts align with skies,
Radiant, where hope lies.

The Watercolor of Wonder

Brush strokes of the dawn,
As colors softly yawn.
Every shade a call,
In the canvas, all.

Rivers run in dreams,
Where nothing's as it seems.
Pinks and blues collide,
Nature's art, our guide.

Clouds in softest gray,
Whisper tales of play.
With every paint-splashed hue,
Life unfolds anew.

In wonder, hearts ignite,
Crafting day from night.
The world sings this song,
In colors, we belong.

Joyful Footprints

In the sand we leave,
Stories to believe.
Each step a melody,
A dance of harmony.

Laughter fills the air,
As sunshine finds us there.
Echoes of delight,
Chasing dreams in flight.

The path of smiles leads,
Through meadows, wild seeds.
Joyfully we roam,
In each heart, a home.

With every step we take,
Memories we make.
In footprints, laughter shines,
Together, love defines.

The Garden of Whimsy

In the garden's glow,
Where the wildflowers grow.
Butterflies in cheer,
Whisper secrets near.

Giggles of the breeze,
Playful as it frees.
Colors boldly play,
In this bright ballet.

With every blooming flower,
Comes the magic power.
To make the heart light,
In the soft twilight.

Where dreams take their flight,
In the fading light.
The garden holds its bliss,
In nature's sweet kiss.

A Celebration of Small Things

In the gentle breeze, leaves sway,
Bright blooms unveil a new display.
A child's laughter in the air,
Moments cherished, memories rare.

Coffee brews in morning light,
Warmth and comfort, pure delight.
Footsteps on a dewy lawn,
Simple pleasures greet the dawn.

A candle flickers, shadows dance,
In every glance, a sweet romance.
Raindrops tap on windowpanes,
Nature's symphony softly reigns.

With open hearts, we pause to see,
The little joys that set us free.
In quiet moments, love unfurls,
A celebration of small worlds.

The Flight of Fancy

Beneath the sky, a dream takes flight,
Whispers of dusk in golden light.
Wings of hope spread wide and far,
Chasing echoes of a distant star.

Each thought a feather in the breeze,
Drifting softly with graceful ease.
Imagination paints the night,
Colorful visions, pure delight.

Clouds become castles, wild and bright,
In a world where dreams ignite.
The moon a lantern, glows above,
Guiding hearts on a path of love.

From the ground, we dare to rise,
Touch the magic in the skies.
In the realm where fancies roam,
We find our hearts, we find our home.

Shimmering Moments

Dappled light through ancient trees,
Twinkling stars in gentle breeze.
Golden hours, a fleeting glance,
Life's sweet rhythm, a sacred dance.

Crimson sunsets brush the shore,
Whispers linger, asking for more.
A child's smile, a lover's sigh,
Shimmering moments passing by.

Frosty dawns and misty nights,
Nature's beauty, endless sights.
Each heartbeat a precious token,
In these moments, hearts are woven.

Let's gather all that gleams and glows,
In every petal, love bestows.
For in the quiet, the loud, the still,
Shimmering moments, they always will.

The Harmony of Heartbeats

In whispered tones, our stories blend,
Each heartbeat sings, a timeless trend.
Connected souls in the twilight's hue,
A symphony of me and you.

In laughter shared, in tears we shed,
The threads of life stretch out, widespread.
Each pulse a rhythm, steady and true,
In every moment, love shines through.

Through life's journey, side by side,
Together we walk, hearts open wide.
Melodies of trust and embrace,
In harmony, we find our place.

Let the music of our hearts play,
Guiding us along the way.
In every heartbeat, strength we find,
The harmony of hearts intertwined.

Beyond the Horizon of Joy

The sun dips low, casting its glow,
Where dreams and laughter freely flow.
In fields of gold, we find our way,
Embracing love in each new day.

With hearts so light, we chase the blue,
Hand in hand, just me and you.
The stars above, they wink and shine,
In this realm, our souls align.

The winds will whisper secrets sweet,
As we dance to a rhythm fleet.
Beyond the horizon, we'll abide,
With hearts as wide as the ocean tide.

In every moment, joy will bloom,
Filling every shadowed room.
Beyond the horizon, hope will fly,
Together we'll dream, you and I.

The Treasure of Time Well Spent

Each moment cherished, a gem displayed,
In laughter shared, the worries fade.
With open hearts, we gather round,
In simple joys, true wealth is found.

Days lost in joy, like whispers soft,
Memories wrap us, lifting aloft.
We weave our stories, thread by thread,
In every word, love's tapestry spread.

Through sunlit paths and starlit skies,
Each heartbeat echoes, time flies by.
In quiet moments, treasures gleam,
When life unfolds just like a dream.

The treasure lies in shared delight,
In fleeting glances, holding tight.
For time is gold when spent with friends,
In laughter's arms, the journey never ends.

Discovering Silver Linings

In cloudy skies where shadows creep,
The heart may ache, but hope won't sleep.
With every storm, a lesson learned,
In darkest nights, a fire burned.

We search for light through every tear,
Finding strength in what we fear.
With every struggle, courage grows,
And silver linings start to show.

When clouds give way to morning light,
We rise anew, embracing bright.
With open eyes, we see the grace,
In every challenge, we find our place.

For though the path may twist and turn,
In every heart, a spark will burn.
Discovering beauty, come what may,
In silver linings, hope will stay.

A Heart Full of Sunshine

In every smile, the warmth we feel,
A tender touch, a love that's real.
With laughter ringing, we chase the day,
In golden rays, our worries sway.

Through stormy clouds, we shine so bright,
With hearts aglow, we ignite the night.
In every shadow, we plant a seed,
A garden sprouting from every deed.

With open arms, we embrace the world,
As dreams unfurl and joy is twirled.
In little moments, we find our grace,
A heart full of sunshine, our sacred space.

Together we journey, hand in hand,
Creating magic with each small strand.
In every heartbeat, love's design,
A canvas painted, a heart full of sunshine.

Festivals of Cheer

Banners dance under skies so blue,
Laughter echoes, joy breaks through.
Colors twirl in the gentle breeze,
Hearts unite, as souls find ease.

Lights aglow in the fading light,
Families gather, what a sight!
Stories shared, old memories reign,
In these moments, love is plain.

Music swells, a charming song,
Every step feels like a throng.
Hands held tight, we spin and sway,
In this festival, we laugh and play.

As night unfolds, stars shine bright,
Our hearts are full, pure delight.
Together we cherish, never apart,
This festival of cheer warms the heart.

The Art of Finding Joy

In simple things, joy takes flight,
A smile shared, a moment's light.
Laughter on a sunlit day,
In tiny wonders, we find our way.

Waves that crash against the shore,
Gentle winds and so much more.
A child's giggle, a lover's glance,
In fleeting moments, we take a chance.

Nature whispers, soft and clear,
Each sunrise brings a brand new cheer.
In every shadow, light will bloom,
In the chaos, find the room.

The art in living, an artist's dream,
Finding joy in every theme.
Through trials faced, we learn to cope,
In the heart's tapestry, we weave hope.

Heartbeats of Elation

In the silence, a heartbeat thumps,
In the joy, it's love that jumps.
A glance exchanged, a sweet embrace,
In every pulse, a sacred space.

Dancing feet on cobblestone,
In every rhythm, we find our own.
The music flows, igniting fire,
With every beat, we rise higher.

Whispers soft, secrets shared,
In tender moments, hearts are bared.
The flood of joy, a tidal wave,
In every breath, we are brave.

Elation sings in a soft refrain,
A tapestry of love's sweet gain.
Together we rise, together we dance,
In this heartbeat, we take a chance.

In Pursuit of the Golden Dawn

Chasing light on the horizon far,
In each sunrise, hope is a star.
Through valleys deep and mountains high,
We seek the day, letting dreams fly.

Morning whispers, shadows fade,
The world awakens, a grand parade.
Colors blend in a vibrant hue,
In this dawn, all feels anew.

Steps we take, with hearts so bold,
Stories waiting to be told.
In each heartbeat, courage born,
We rise together, seek the dawn.

The golden glow, like a promise made,
In shared journeys, fears cascade.
Together we flourish, together we soar,
In pursuit of dreams, forevermore.

The Search for Bliss

In the garden where shadows play,
I seek the light of a brighter day.
Petals open with soft grace,
Each moment a gentle embrace.

Dreams like rivers flowing wide,
Chasing hopes I cannot hide.
Through valleys deep, I wander far,
Following the glow of a distant star.

A whisper calls from the hidden glen,
Inviting me back to begin again.
With every step, my heart takes flight,
In the pursuit of pure delight.

Beneath the sky, both vast and blue,
I find the path that leads to you.
Bliss awaits, just out of sight,
Guided by the soft moonlight.

Trails of Contentment

Along the winding forest trail,
Gentle breezes start to sail.
Leaves dance lightly to the ground,
In this quiet, peace is found.

Streams of laughter fill the air,
Echoes of joy beyond compare.
Sunset paints the sky with gold,
Stories of love in silence told.

Each step reveals the world's sweet song,
Reminds me where I truly belong.
Nature's canvas, rich and bright,
Fills my heart with pure delight.

On these trails, I take a breath,
Embracing life, welcoming depth.
Contentment nestled in my soul,
A soothing balm that makes me whole.

Whispers of Joy

In the morning light, a bird sings,
Joy is found in simple things.
A child's laughter, a blooming rose,
Each moment blossoms as it grows.

Whispers of joy float on the breeze,
Dancing softly among the trees.
Every heartbeat, a rhythmic tune,
Filling our lives with endless boon.

Stars will twinkle in the night,
Guiding thoughts towards pure delight.
In dreams alive, our spirits play,
Whispers of joy, leading the way.

Together we walk this vibrant path,
Sharing stories, igniting laughter's wrath.
In the tapestry of life, thread by thread,
Whispers of joy are gently spread.

Mapping the Smile

With every sunrise, a map unfolds,
A journey of smiles that life beholds.
Tracing paths where laughter flows,
In the heart, a garden grows.

Each gentle smile is like a star,
Illuminating how loved we are.
Moments captured, bright and meek,
Mapping the joy that words can't speak.

With friends beside, the world feels light,
Every shared glance, a pure delight.
In this adventure, hand in hand,
Mapping the smile across the land.

Through valleys low and mountains high,
We find the joy that makes us fly.
In every hug, in every tear,
Mapping our smiles, love draws near.

Journey to the Sunlight

In the dawn's embrace, I rise,
Wings unfurling, touching skies.
Each step leads to warmth ahead,
A path where dreams and hopes are fed.

Through valleys deep and mountains high,
I chase the glow where shadows lie.
With every heartbeat, I'm anew,
A journey paved in golden hue.

The whispers guide me, gentle, clear,
In every corner, joy is near.
The sunlight calls, I cannot sway,
To brighter lands, I find my way.

With faith as fuel, I shall arrive,
In radiant worlds, I'll surely thrive.
The journey's end is just the start,
For sunlight lives within my heart.

Whispers of Joy in the Breeze

Dancing leaves upon the trees,
Softly swaying in the breeze.
Every rustle tells a tale,
Of laughter sweet, of love that sails.

Sunbeams glimmer, shadows play,
Nature sings in bright array.
With every breath, the world unveils,
The magic in its whispered trails.

Joy lingers on the evening air,
Memories woven with tender care.
In every sigh the plants release,
A gentle promise, endless peace.

Amidst the softness, hearts align,
Connected souls in love, divine.
Forever grateful for the sound,
Of joy in breezes all around.

The Elusive Smile

A glimmer here, a flicker there,
The elusive smile seems so rare.
Like fleeting shadows in the night,
It dances just beyond my sight.

With every turn, I seek its glow,
Through every high and every low.
In laughter shared, its essence thrives,
A spark of joy that still survives.

Moments cherished, sweet and bright,
Each whisper calls, a soft invite.
To catch that smile, to hold it near,
A treasure found, forever dear.

Yet even when it slips away,
The warmth remains, come what may.
In every heartbeat, in every style,
The world ignites with that sweet smile.

Chasing Radiance

Through hidden paths of dreams untold,
I chase the radiance, brave and bold.
With every step, the light grows close,
In shadows deep, my heart will boast.

The morning sun begins to rise,
Painting gold upon the skies.
Each flicker sings a vibrant tune,
A dance of hope, a brightened rune.

I wander where the wildflowers sway,
Embracing colors on display.
With eyes alight, the journey calls,
To break the chains, to rise, to fall.

With every heartbeat, I will strive,
To feel the spark, to feel alive.
In chasing radiance, I find it true,
The light I seek is born anew.

A Journey to Radiance

In shadows deep, we seek the light,
With every step, our hearts take flight.
The dawn awakens, dreams anew,
As hope cascades in vibrant hue.

Through valleys low and mountains high,
We chase the stars that grace the sky.
Each challenge faced, a lesson learned,
With every turn, the fire burns.

The path is winding, yet we tread,
With courage strong and spirits fed.
A dance of light on ocean's crest,
Together found, we are our best.

As twilight falls, the stars align,
In unity, our souls combine.
The journey's end, a radiant smile,
For love and joy, we walk this mile.

The Road to Serendipity

With every step, a tale unfolds,
Unseen treasures, fortunes told.
In laughter shared, the moments bloom,
A chance encounter lights the room.

Through winding lanes and paths unknown,
The heart finds joy when seeds are sown.
Each twist and turn, a dance of fate,
In whispered dreams, we resonate.

Chasing echoes down the way,
We find the magic in the play.
In fleeting glances, sparks ignite,
As serendipity takes flight.

The road ahead, with wonder lined,
In every heart, a treasure find.
With open arms, the world to greet,
We walk together, spirits sweet.

Chasing Golden Moments

In sunrise hues, we make a wish,
To seize the day, to live, to kiss.
Each second flows like rivers wide,
In golden moments, we confide.

With laughter bright, we paint the sky,
In fleeting time, we learn to fly.
The petals fall, the seasons change,
Yet love remains, the heart's exchange.

Through laughter's tones and whispers sweet,
We sprint along, our hearts in beat.
In memories, both old and new,
The golden glow brings joy in view.

So raise a glass to times we share,
In every glance, in every stare.
With open hearts, we chase the sun,
In golden moments, we are one.

Echoes of Elation

In twilight's glow, the laughter rings,
A joyful song that spirit sings.
With every cheer, a memory made,
In elation's grasp, we are arrayed.

Through gardens bright and fields of green,
We dance in rhythms, pure, unseen.
Each echo builds, a vibrant choir,
In hearts that soar, in dreams that fire.

Together bound in blissful flight,
With open hearts, we claim the night.
In every hug, in every tear,
The echoes whisper, love draws near.

At journey's end, we hold it tight,
The warmth we found, a shared delight.
As echoes fade, they leave a trace,
In every heart, the joy's embrace.

The Odyssey of Cheer

In distant lands, the laughter sails,
Bright hearts unite, as joy prevails.
Waves of mirth, the song we sing,
Hopeful whispers, the new dawn brings.

Each step we take, the light we chase,
Smiles weaving through time and space.
Together we wander, hand in hand,
Crafting dreams, like castles in sand.

Through valleys deep, and mountains high,
Chasing rainbows across the sky.
With every heartbeat, we set forth,
An odyssey of cheer, our worth.

When shadows fall and skies grow gray,
We'll light the path, come what may.
In unity, our spirits soar,
Forevermore, we'll seek the shore.

Pathways to Euphoria

In gentle breezes, joy takes flight,
Beneath the stars, we find our light.
Every moment, a sweet embrace,
Together we wander, heartbeats race.

Through fields of dreams, our spirits dance,
In laughter's glow, we take a chance.
We build our steps on hope and grace,
On pathways paved with love's warm trace.

With every heartbeat, sparks ignite,
In harmony, we chase the night.
A tapestry of vibrant hues,
In euphoria, we'll never lose.

So let us journey without fear,
For in our hearts, joy perseveres.
Hand in hand, we'll find the way,
On pathways to forever stay.

Dancing with the Sun

Awake with dawn, the world in bloom,
Nature's stage, banishing gloom.
With every ray, our spirits rise,
In sunlit dreams, we touch the skies.

Through fields of gold, we sway and twirl,
In gentle warmth, the light unfurl.
Together we sway, a joyous run,
In this embrace, we dance with the sun.

Each golden hour, a treasure dear,
Chasing shadows, we conquer fear.
In rhythm wild, our hearts align,
With every beat, our souls entwine.

In twilight's glow, we'll not retreat,
For in this dance, we find our beat.
So let us celebrate, and be one,
In joyful light, we're dancing with the sun.

The Secret Garden of Laughter

Beyond the gate, a world awaits,
Where laughter hides and joy creates.
In blossoms bloom, our spirits play,
In secret gardens, we find our way.

With whispered jokes, the petals sway,
In this embrace, we choose to stay.
Every giggle, a fragrant breeze,
In cherished moments, time will freeze.

Through winding paths, we share our dreams,
In hidden nooks, the magic gleams.
Together we plant, with hopeful tears,
A garden rich with love and cheers.

So let us wander, hand in hand,
In laughter's tune, forever stand.
For in this sanctuary divine,
The secret garden will always shine.

The Treasure of Inner Peace

In quiet corners, whispers dwell,
A gentle calm, where dreamers tell.
Each breath a balm, a soft release,
Within the soul lies inner peace.

Through tangled thoughts, the heart can roam,
In stillness found, we make our home.
Let go of storms that never cease,
Embrace the joy, the warmth, the peace.

Like morning dew on blades of grass,
We find our way, we watch time pass.
With every step, our worries cease,
In nature's arms, we find our peace.

In each soft sigh, in every smile,
We gather strength, we walk each mile.
The treasure waits, an endless lease,
A journey sweet, our inner peace.

Serendipity's Embrace

A chance encounter, a fleeting glance,
The world unfolds in a sweet dance.
Paths intertwined, fate's gentle lace,
We find our way in serendipity's embrace.

Moments cherished, unexpected grace,
A smile that lights up a solemn face.
In laughter shared, in time's warm trace,
We paint our lives in serendipity's embrace.

The whisper of fate, a guiding hand,
Leads us softly to promised land.
In every stumble, there's a place,
To bask in joy, in serendipity's embrace.

With open hearts, we learn to see,
The beauty found in what might be.
In every turn, we find our pace,
Together held in serendipity's embrace.

Dancing with Shadows of Light

In twilight's glow, the dancers play,
With shadows long, they sway and sway.
A gentle step, a fleeting sight,
We dance along with shadows of light.

In every flicker, a story glows,
As nightfall deepens, our heartbeat flows.
With whispered dreams taking flight,
We embrace the dance of shadows of light.

The music sighs, a soft refrain,
With every pause, we feel the gain.
In perfect unison, we ignite,
Our souls entwined in shadows of light.

The rhythm calls, the stars ignite,
Together we chase the waning night.
In every twirl, our spirits height,
We find our joy in shadows of light.

The Map of Merriment

With laughter's ink, we sketch the day,
A map of joy, in bright array.
Turn every corner, seek delight,
In the map of merriment, pure and bright.

Through valleys deep and mountains high,
With each new dawn, our spirits fly.
In hidden nooks, where laughter's right,
We trace our path on merriment's map tonight.

In gentle whispers and playful tease,
We find the joy that sets us free.
With every smile, our hearts unite,
As we explore the map of merriment's light.

So gather round, let stories blend,
In joyful moments that never end.
With every step, in love's invite,
We chart the course on merriment's map, so bright.

The Compendium of Joyful Journeys

In fields where laughter blooms so bright,
We chase the sun until it's night.
With every step, we dance and sing,
Joy is the treasure, the heart's offering.

Through mountains high and valleys low,
We find the paths where kindness flows.
Together, hand in hand we roam,
In every heart, we've found a home.

The rivers sparkle, weaving fate,
In every moment, love's our slate.
Adventure calls us, wild and free,
The journey itself is our decree.

So here we write this joyful tome,
Each memory a cherished poem.
For life is grand, the stories spun,
In this compendium, we're all one.

The Pursuit of Joy

We seek the smile in morning's grace,
In tiny moments, we find our place.
With open hearts and eyes so wide,
In every glance, we feel joy's tide.

Through laughter shared and kindness shown,
The seeds of happiness are sown.
In every challenge, a chance to grow,
In every tear, a new joy's glow.

We wander paths both near and far,
In the mind's eye, we see the star.
With every step, we write the score,
A symphony of joy to explore.

So let us chase the fading light,
In every shadow, find what's bright.
In unity, let's pave the way,
For in the pursuit, joy likes to stay.

The Compass of Delight

With joy as compass, we set the sail,
In every heart, we share the tale.
Through storms and calm, we'll navigate,
Delight awaits, let's celebrate.

In every sunrise, a fresh new start,
The map of life drawn on the heart.
With laughter guiding, we chart the seas,
Filling our sails with gentle breeze.

Together we'll traverse the unknown,
With every step, a bond has grown.
In every whisper of the night,
Delight unveils a world so bright.

So here we stand, with spirits high,
Side by side as time drifts by.
With joy as compass, we'll find our way,
In the journey of life, come what may.

Finding the Light Within

In quiet moments, still and deep,
We breathe in peace, our souls to keep.
The light within begins to glow,
A gentle warmth that we all know.

In shadows cast by doubt and fear,
We search for love that feels so near.
With every heartbeat, truths unwind,
In every whisper, hope's defined.

The journey inward leads us home,
Through winding paths where hearts will roam.
In every heart, a spark ignites,
Finding the light in darkest nights.

So let the beacon guide our way,
In every dawn, we blend and sway.
For in this quest, we learn and grow,
Finding the light, our spirits glow.

Mornings Heavy with Wonder

In dawn's embrace, the world awakes,
Mist dances lightly over the lakes.
Birds sing softly, a sweet refrain,
Hope lingers gently after the rain.

Golden rays peek through the trees,
Nature hums softly on the breeze.
Each moment whispers, time stands still,
Awash in wonder, hearts are filled.

The day unfurls like petals in bloom,
Casting light on shadows, lifting gloom.
In every heartbeat, dreams ignite,
Morning unveils the beauty of light.

Through quiet breath, we find our place,
In every dawn, a fleeting grace.
Mornings heavy with a soft glow,
Remind us gently to feel and grow.

Journeys Under Starlit Skies

Under a canopy of endless night,
Dreams take flight, hearts feel light.
Whispers of galaxies, secrets shared,
In this vast tapestry, souls are bared.

Footsteps on paths less traveled,
Each turn a mystery unraveled.
Moonbeams guide with silver threads,
Woven tales of the wanderers' beds.

With every star, a wish is cast,
Adventures beckon, shadows past.
To roam the world, both far and near,
Echoes of laughter filled with cheer.

Journeys guided by the cosmos' grace,
Finding home in each sacred space.
Under starlit skies, dreams unfurl,
In the night's embrace, we find our pearl.

The Flavor of Joy

Sweet as honey, laughter blooms,
Filling hearts, dispelling glooms.
In every smile, a spark ignites,
Painting memories, pure delights.

Sunshine sprinkling through the trees,
Joy flows gently on the breeze.
Colors dance in vibrant hues,
Moments cherished, never to lose.

With every heartbeat, a song is sung,
In the essence of life, we are young.
Sharing dreams under the sun's glow,
Savoring every taste of joy we know.

The flavor of joy, a sweet refrain,
Filling us up time and again.
In simple things, we find our cheer,
In the warmth of love, we persevere.

Stitches of Laughter

Threads of joy weave through the air,
Laughter sparkles, moments rare.
Each giggle stitches hearts so tight,
In the fabric of life, pure delight.

Shared stories echo, soft and sweet,
Binding us closer, a rhythmic beat.
In each chuckle, memories bloom,
Filling our lives with love's perfume.

With every joke, spirits rise high,
Casting aside clouds in the sky.
Like a warm quilt on a winter's night,
Laughter surrounds us, feels just right.

Stitch by stitch, we sew our days,
In laughter's embrace, we find our ways.
Together we stand, hand in hand,
In the tapestry of life, forever grand.

The Skylark's Song

In the dawn, the lark takes flight,
Melodies fill the morning light.
Dancing high in skies so blue,
　Nature's choir sings anew.

With each note, the world awakes,
Joyful hearts, as wonder breaks.
Wings spread wide, the spirit soars,
Freedom found where beauty pours.

Fields below, in blossoms bright,
　Echo laughter, pure delight.
　　In a symphony of peace,
All our troubles find release.

As the sun begins to set,
Whispers soft, we won't forget.
The skylark's song will always stay,
　Guiding hope along the way.

Footprints in Fields of Laughter

In the fields where children play,
Footprints left in bright array.
Laughter dances near and far,
Joyful echoes, like a star.

Summer sun and skies so wide,
Chasing dreams, we run and hide.
Every step a story told,
In the warmth, our hearts unfold.

Breezes carry whispers sweet,
Joyful moments, life's retreat.
In the grass, where memories bloom,
Footprints linger, dispelling gloom.

As twilight casts its golden glow,
Laughter fades, yet love will grow.
In the silence, echoes remain,
Footprints in laughter, wistful gain.

The Canvas of Contentment

In the quiet of the day,
Colors blend in soft array.
Every stroke, a gentle sigh,
Life, a canvas, as we try.

Brush of kindness, touch of grace,
Moments painted, time can't erase.
Hues of hope and dreams serene,
On this canvas, pure and clean.

Sunset glows with amber rays,
Casting light on varied ways.
Each heartbeat, a stroke so fine,
Crafting life's design divine.

In stillness, peace will find,
A masterpiece within the mind.
The canvas waits, our hearts in tune,
Creating beauty 'neath the moon.

Singing with the Stars

Underneath a velvet sky,
Stars awaken, whisper why.
In their glow, we find our dance,
Singing dreams in sweet romance.

Galaxies, in twinkling light,
Guide us through the endless night.
With each note, the cosmos sways,
In harmony, our spirits play.

Voices rise like shooting stars,
Echoes carried, near and far.
In the silence, hearts align,
Singing with the stars, divine.

As dawn approaches, colors blend,
Songs of night begin to end.
Yet in our hearts, a flame remains,
Singing softly, love sustains.

Milton Keynes UK
Ingram Content Group UK Ltd.
UKHW051811101024
449294UK00007BA/62